394	Add 100	
2789	Subtract 1000	
8994	Add 10	

505	Subtract 10	
4098	Add 1000	
3090	Subtract 100	

(6653)   (8082)   (6975)   (7528)   (2297)   (6491)

Write the number which has

8 tens _____   5 hundreds _____   2 units _____

thousands digit 6 **and** tens digit 9. _____

Write True (T) **or** False (F) for each example.

5094 > 3689 ___   7510 < 6988 ___   9550 < 9555 ___

Write in order. Start with the largest number.

{ 7695 }   { 5976 }   { 9765 }   { 5796 }   { 6957 }

_____   _____   _____   _____   _____

Write in **numerals**.

Six thousand _____   Nine thousand and ten _____

Four thousand seven hundred and fifty-two _____

Write in **words**.

5500 _____

40th _____   100th _____

Numbers to 10 000: Textbook pages 4–8

Check-up 3

About how many metres has each arrow travelled?

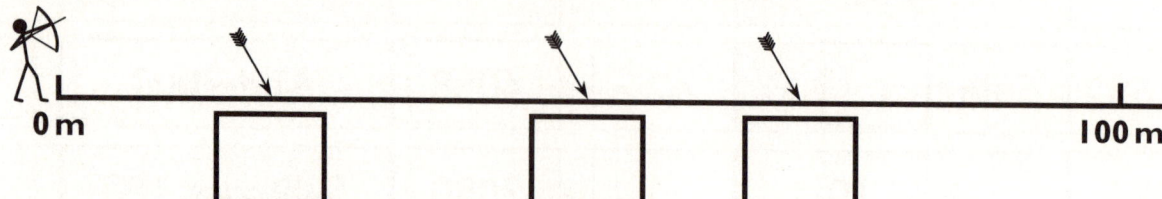

About how many millilitres are in each jar?

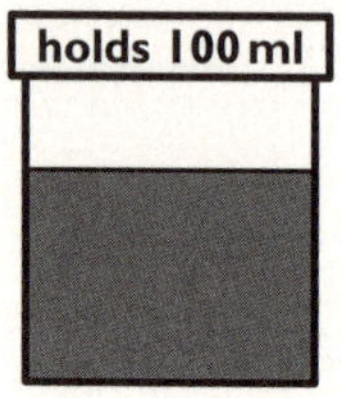

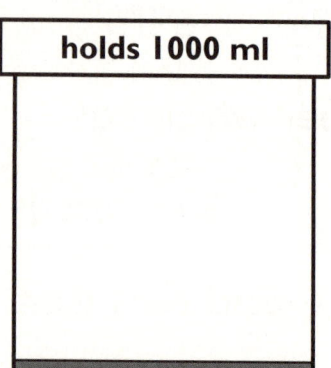

Write to the **nearest hundred**.

234 → ☐   86 → ☐   975 → ☐

Write to the **nearest ten**.

418 → ☐   503 → ☐   745 → ☐

Write the distance from Anna's house to Sam's house

- to the nearest hundred metres ____
- to the nearest ten metres. ____

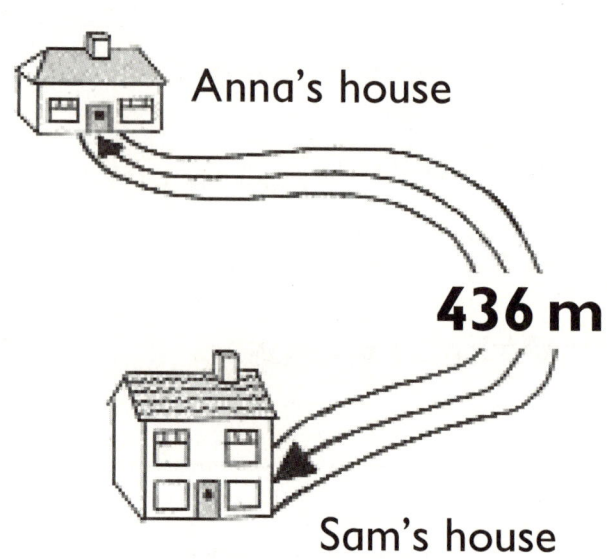

Anna's house

436 m

Sam's house

Numbers to 10 000: Textbook pages 9–10

Check-up 4

Double each number.

23 → ☐   42 → ☐   34 → ☐
36 → ☐   29 → ☐   47 → ☐

34 + 33 = ☐   18 + 19 = ☐   27 + 28 = ☐
23 + 21 = ☐   37 + 39 = ☐   45 + 47 = ☐

Find each total.

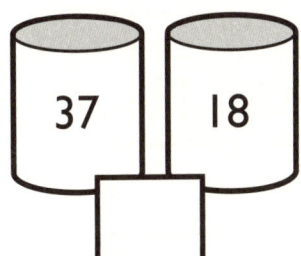
37 18

46 39

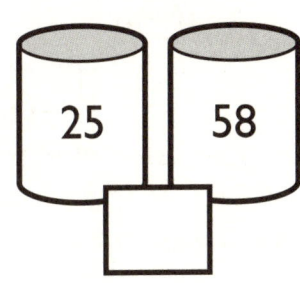
25 58

54 + 17 = ☐   26 + 19 = ☐   25 + 37 = ☐
28 + ☐ = 57   ☐ + 17 = 62   36 + ☐ = 92

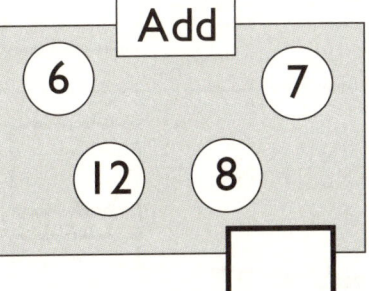

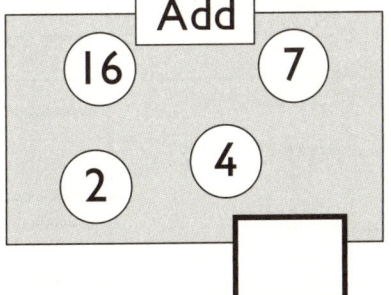

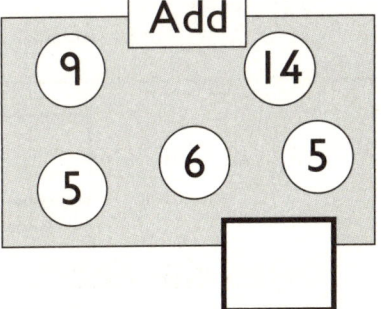

11 + 9 + 6 + ☐ = 30   13 + ☐ + 12 + 3 = 35

Addition to 1000: Textbook pages 11–13

Check-up 5

90 + 40 = ☐   50 + 80 = ☐   60 + 70 = ☐

76 + 50 = ☐   89 + 30 = ☐   80 + 65 = ☐

93 + ☐ = 113   ☐ + 60 = 128   79 + ☐ = 119

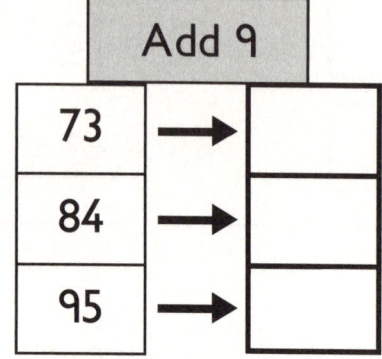
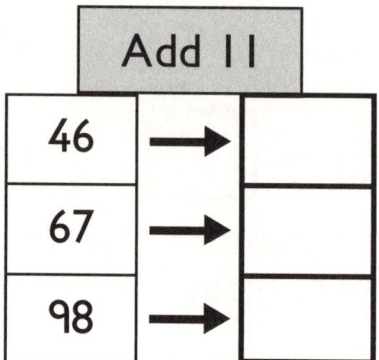
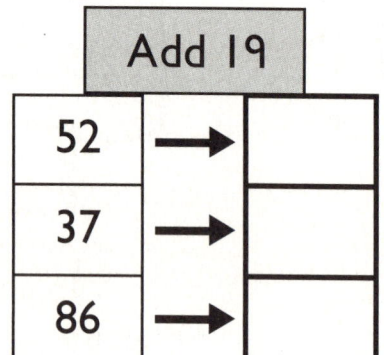
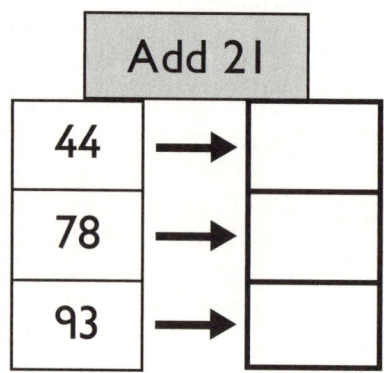

93 + 41 = ☐   85 + 29 = ☐   74 + 59 = ☐

76 + 62 = ☐   54 + 68 = ☐   97 + 42 = ☐

64 + 53 = ☐   92 + 47 = ☐   52 + 84 = ☐

73 + 68 = ☐   87 + 45 = ☐   66 + 77 = ☐

64 + ☐ = 138   39 + ☐ = 115

Addition to 1000: Textbook pages 15–17

Check-up 6

Find each total amount.

£460 £30 [ ]
£70 £610 [ ]
£228 £41 [ ]
£366 £29 [ ]
£580 £90 [ ]
£60 £770 [ ]

Double each number.

400 → ____   150 → ____   350 → ____

Make 1000.

200 + [ ]   650 + [ ]   850 + [ ]
[ ] + 250   [ ] + 300   [ ] + 450

Double each number.

230 → ____   410 → ____   160 → ____   370 → ____

340 + 330 = [ ]   260 + 270 = [ ]   490 + 480 = [ ]

340 + [ ] = 400   545 + [ ] = 600
[ ] + 208 = 300   [ ] + 673 = 700

Addition to 1000: Textbook pages 18–21

Check-up 7

63 – 21 = ___   97 – 51 = ___   95 – 82 = ___

54 – 19 = ___   72 – 39 = ___   81 – 68 = ___

Subtract 48 from 86. ___   99 minus 72 = ___

70 take away 32 = ___   Take 27 from 53. ___

---

92 – 3 = ___   46 – 9 = ___   53 – 5 = ___

31 – 8 = ___   62 – 4 = ___   84 – 7 = ___

73 – ☐ = 66   ☐ – 6 = 89

A £73   B £64   C £40   D £25

What is the price difference between

Pot B and Pot C ____   Pot A and Pot B ____

Pot D and Pot B ____   Pot D and Pot A? ____

Each price is reduced by £18. Find the **new** price of

Pot A ____   Pot B ____

---

53 – ☐ = 35   82 – ☐ = 45

Subtraction to 1000: Textbook pages 25–26

Check-up 8

How much does each have left?

Tula saved £105.
She spent £7.

_____ left.

Will saved £200.
He spent £6.

_____ left.

Tara saved £403.
She spent £9.

_____ left.

Hank saved £144.
He spent £8.

_____ left.

Subtract 5 from 641. _____   423 minus 7 _____

4 less than 302 _____   821 subtract 3 _____

Take 9 from 250. _____   510 take away 6 _____

Match.

160 – 30		548	840		758 – 41
567 – 19		541	717		765 – 29
572 – 31		130	736		900 – 60

---

141 – 60 = ____   116 – 30 = ____   123 – 50 = ____

106 – 14 = ____   105 – 11 = ____   114 – 17 = ____

123 – 32 = ____   116 – 28 = ____   126 – 37 = ____

106 – ☐ = 88   112 – ☐ = 83   122 – ☐ = 86

Subtraction: Textbook pages 29–30

Check-up 9

Subtract 90 from 250. _____   Take 80 from 310. _____

320 minus 110 _____   580 subtract 160 _____

130 take away 50 _____   400 subtract 130 _____

230 – ☐ = 110   380 – ☐ = 240   690 – ☐ = 520

Find the difference between

96 and 103 _____   105 and 99 _____   95 and 101 _____

197 and 204 _____   202 and 198 _____   294 and 303 _____

98 and 113 _____   205 and 187 _____   295 and 312 _____

483   356   683   363
550   665   283   490

Choose two numbers with a difference of

• 200 _____ _____   • 7 _____ _____

• 60 _____ _____   • 18 _____ _____

How much did each person **start** with?
Sue spent £17.   Ian spent £140.
She had £188 left. _____   He had £330 left. _____

Subtraction: Textbook pages 31–33

Check-up 10

2 × 7 = ☐   3 × 5 = ☐   10 × 4 = ☐

9 × 3 = ☐   5 × 8 = ☐   0 × 2 = ☐

4 × 4 = ☐   7 × 3 = ☐   4 × 8 = ☐

3 × ☐ = 18   4 × ☐ = 28   5 × ☐ = 35

☐ × 10 = 70   ☐ × 2 = 18   ☐ × 3 = 3

4 × ☐ = 20   3 × ☐ = 30   5 × ☐ = 0

Find the cost of

three 🍎 _____   four 🍌 _____

five 🍌 and two 🍊 _____

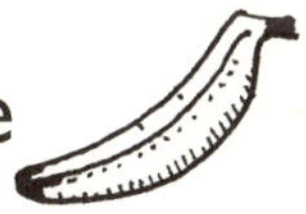

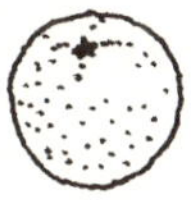

10 × 73 = ☐   160 × 10 = ☐   10 × 317 = ☐

100 × 7 = ☐   100 × 39 = ☐   50 × 100 = ☐

10 × ☐ = 180   10 × ☐ = 7300

100 × ☐ = 900   100 × ☐ = 3600

Multiplication: Textbook pages 38–39

Check-up 11

8 × 5 = ☐   6 sevens = ☐   8 × 8 = ☐

8 times 4 = ☐   6 × 6 = ☐   10 × 6 = ☐

2 × 8 = ☐   8 nines = ☐   6 times 8 = ☐

5 × 6 = ☐   6 × 0 = ☐   3 × 8 = ☐

Match.

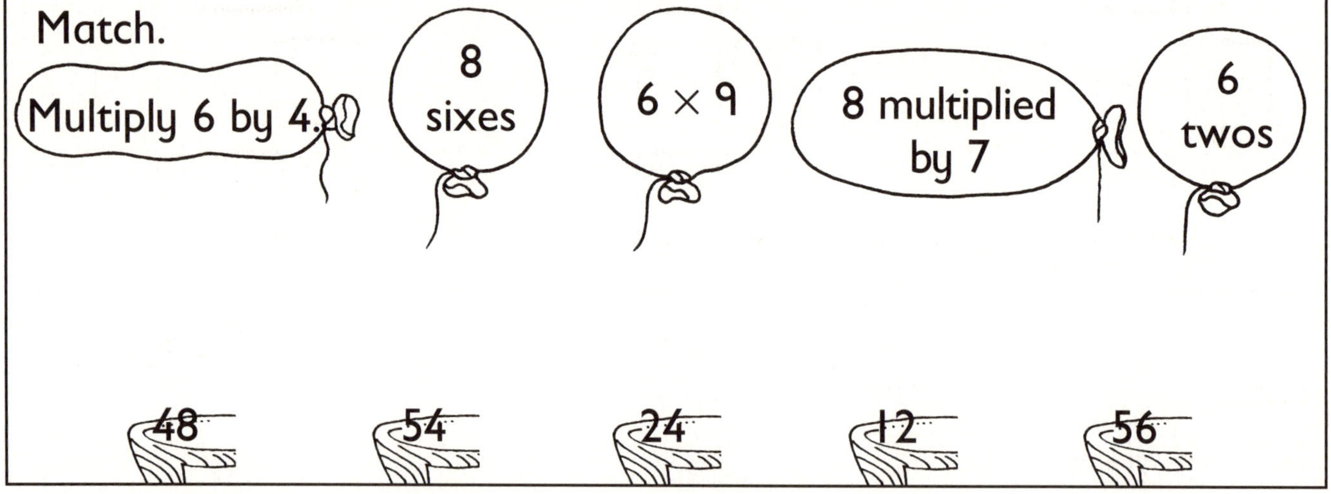

Multiply 6 by 4.   8 sixes   6 × 9   8 multiplied by 7   6 twos

48   54   24   12   56

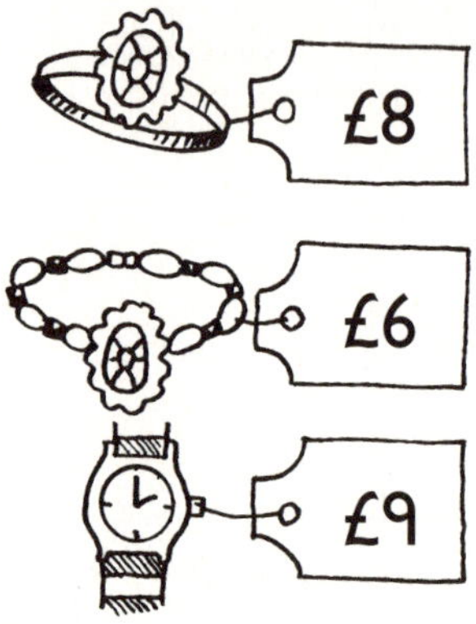

Find the cost of

seven

six

eight

 £8
£6
£9

6 × ☐ = 18   8 × ☐ = 0   8 × ☐ = 64

☐ × 8 = 8   ☐ × 6 = 36   ☐ × 10 = 80

6 × ☐ = 42   ☐ × 8 = 24   6 × ☐ = 6

Multiplication: Textbook pages 40–41

Check-up 12

9 × 9 = ☐   9 × 5 = ☐   2 × 9 = ☐
9 × 6 = ☐   7 × 8 = ☐   7 × 6 = ☐
7 × 10 = ☐ 9 × 4 = ☐   7 × 9 = ☐
7 × 5 = ☐   3 × 7 = ☐   9 × 0 = ☐

How many apples are in

9 bags ___   6 bags ___   8 bags ___   7 bags? ___

How many plums are in

8 bags ___   7 bags ___   9 bags ___   6 bags? ___

Write True (T) or False (F) for each example.

7 fours = 28 ___   7 multiplied by 7 is 48. ___

7 zeros = 0 ___   9 tens = 90 ___

9 times 3 = 27 ___   9 times 8 is 81. ___

7 × ☐ = 35   7 × ☐ = 7   7 × ☐ = 63
☐ × 2 = 14   ☐ × 4 = 36   ☐ × 1 = 9
9 × ☐ = 63   7 × ☐ = 28   9 × ☐ = 45

Multiplication: Textbook pages 42–43

Check-up 13

 £39    £35    £23    £17

Find the cost of

two  ☐   four  ☐

three 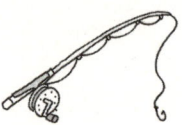 ☐   five  ☐

five  ☐   twenty 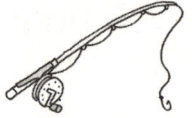 ☐

90 crackers   60 balloons   80 candles   70 hats

How many in

5 boxes of hats ☐   4 boxes of candles ☐

3 boxes of balloons ☐   2 boxes of crackers? ☐

Find the **approximate** cost of

5 masks ☐    49p

4 radios. ☐    £31

Find Zara's starting number.

 I add 6 and multiply by 4. My answer is 100.   ☐

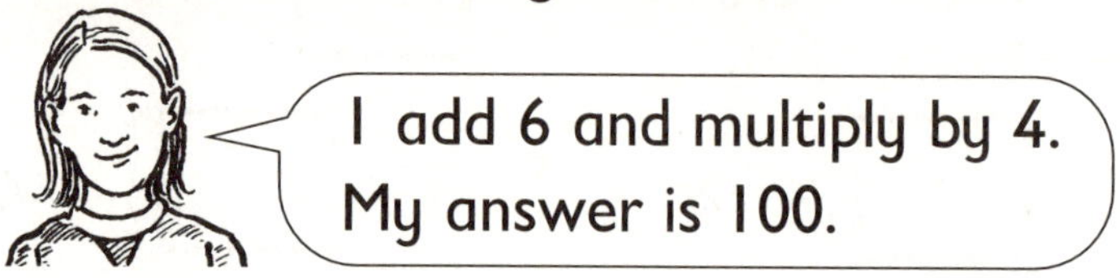

Multiplication: Textbook pages 45–47

Check-up 14

Each buggy holds 8 children.

How many buggies are needed to hold

    [48]

____ buggies   ____ buggies   ____ buggies

Divide 40 by 8. ____   Share 24 equally among 8. ____

0 divided by 8 ____   How many eights make 72? ____

Divide 80 by 8. ____   Group 56 in eights. ____

8 divided by 8 ____   Divide 16 equally among 8. ____

☐ ÷ 8 = 6   ☐ ÷ 8 = 3   ☐ ÷ 8 = 7

☐ ÷ 8 = 10   ☐ ÷ 8 = 0   ☐ ÷ 8 = 4

72 children form teams of 8 for rounders.

How many teams are there? ____

40 children play football in teams of 8.

How many teams are there? ____

Division: Textbook page 51

Check-up 15

Six children can sit in a banana boat.
How many boats are needed for these children?

(a) 36   (b) 48   (c) 24

___ boats   ___ boats   ___ boats

60 divided by 6 ___   How many sixes make 30? ___

Divide 12 by 6. ___   Share 6 equally among 6. ___

Divide 54 by 6. ___   How many groups of 6 are in 18? ___

42 divided by 6 ___   Divide 0 equally among 6. ___

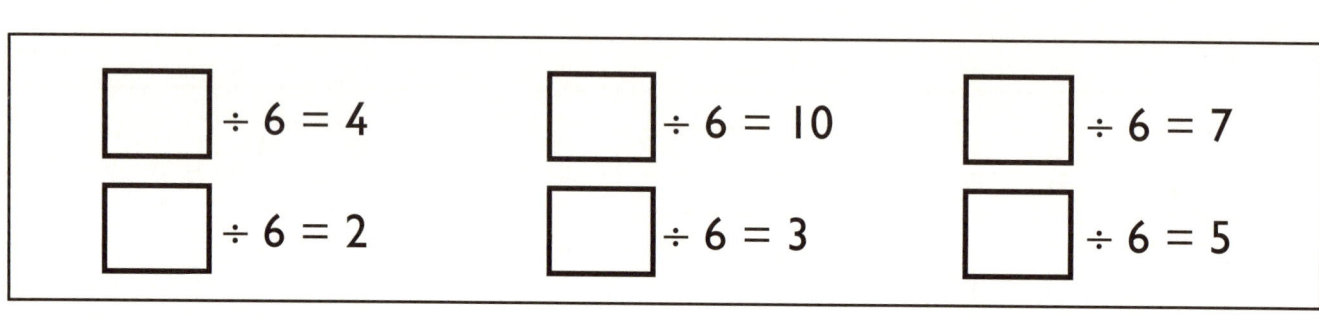

☐ ÷ 6 = 4   ☐ ÷ 6 = 10   ☐ ÷ 6 = 7

☐ ÷ 6 = 2   ☐ ÷ 6 = 3   ☐ ÷ 6 = 5

Gemma spent 36p on tickets. She bought twice as many tickets for the Chutes as she did for the Skytrain.

How many tickets did she buy

for the Chutes ___

for the Skytrain? ___

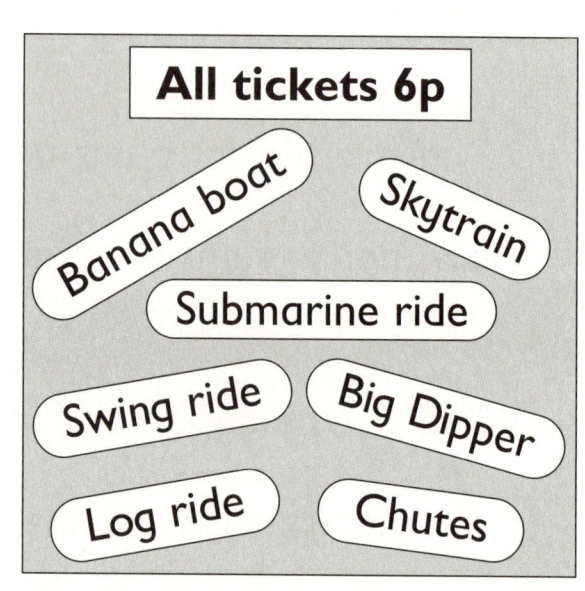

All tickets 6p

Banana boat, Skytrain, Submarine ride, Swing ride, Big Dipper, Log ride, Chutes

Division: Textbook page 52

Check-up 16

Oranges are sold in nets of 9.
How many nets are needed for

45 oranges ☐

81 oranges ☐

27 oranges ☐   90 oranges ☐   63 oranges? ☐

How many nines make 36? ☐   Divide 9 by 9. ☐

Share 18 equally among 9. ☐   Zero divided by 9 ☐

Divide 54 equally among 9. ☐   Divide 72 by 9. ☐

27 ÷ 9 = ☐   81 ÷ 9 = ☐   0 ÷ 9 = ☐

☐ ÷ 9 = 7   ☐ ÷ 9 = 1   ☐ ÷ 9 = 10

How many oranges can you buy when you spend

36p ☐   72p ☐   54p? ☐

9p each

Division: Textbook page 53

Check-up 17

Share these sweets equally among 7 children.

35  → ☐ each

63 → ☐ each

49 → ☐ each

7 → ☐ each

Group 28 in sevens. ☐   0 divided by 7 ☐

Share 14 equally among 7. ☐   Divide 70 by 7. ☐

Divide 56 equally among 7. ☐ 42 divided by 7 ☐

---

21 ÷ 7 = ☐   49 ÷ 7 = ☐   0 ÷ 7 = ☐

☐ ÷ 7 = 5   ☐ ÷ 7 = 9   ☐ ÷ 7 = 1

How many packets of FFizzers can you buy when you spend

21p ☐   70p ☐   42p ☐   56p? ☐

Division: Textbook page 54

Check-up 18

Miss Murray spent £42 on maths books.
The books cost £6 each.
How many maths books did she buy? ☐

Complete.

	Cities	Farms	Castles	Transport
Miss Murray spent ...	£54	£63	£72	£60
Each book cost ...	£9	£7	£8	£6
Number of books bought				

How many groups of nine make 36? ☐   Divide 0 by 7. ☐

Divide 24 equally among 8. ☐   48 divided by 6 ☐

Share 80 equally among 8. ☐   Divide 42 by 7. ☐

45 ÷ 9 = ☐   6 ÷ 6 = ☐   56 ÷ 8 = ☐

☐ ÷ 7 = 5   ☐ ÷ 9 = 8   ☐ ÷ 8 = 4

18 ÷ ☐ = 3   63 ÷ ☐ = 7   56 ÷ ☐ = 8

Division: Textbook page 55

Check-up 19

How much money does each child have?

Write these amounts in order, starting with the **smallest**.

£20·07   £20·00   £19·80   £19·08

List notes and coins for each amount. Use as few as possible.

£16·33

£30·86

Write each amount in **pounds and pence**.

972p   4627p   8304p

Write each amount in **pence**.

£3·99   £52·63   £70·60

Round each amount **to the nearest pound**.

£23·80   £49·19   £36·47

Money: Textbook pages 61–62

Check-up 20

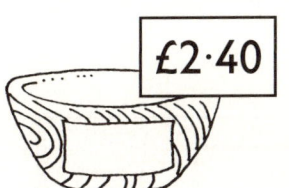 £2·40  £1·30  £1·70  70p  90p

Find the total cost of

- a bowl, a plate and a giraffe _____

- a mask, a giraffe and a plate _____

- a statue, a bowl, a mask and a giraffe. _____

£1·30 + ☐ = £2·70   £2·70 + ☐ = £3·60

£1·60 + ☐ = £2·30   £2·50 + ☐ = £4·00

 £1·45   £2·25

Find the total cost of

- a necklace and a bracelet _____
- two bracelets _____
- a ring and a necklace _____
- a bracelet and a brooch _____
- a brooch and a ring. _____

£1·12   £2·33

Pam had a £20 note. She bought a book costing £13·40.
List the coins and notes in her change.

_____

Zoe paid for a T-shirt with a £20 note.
Her change was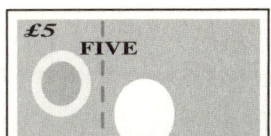

How much did she spend? _____

Money: Textbook pages 63–65

Check-up 21

Colour.

$2\frac{1}{3}$

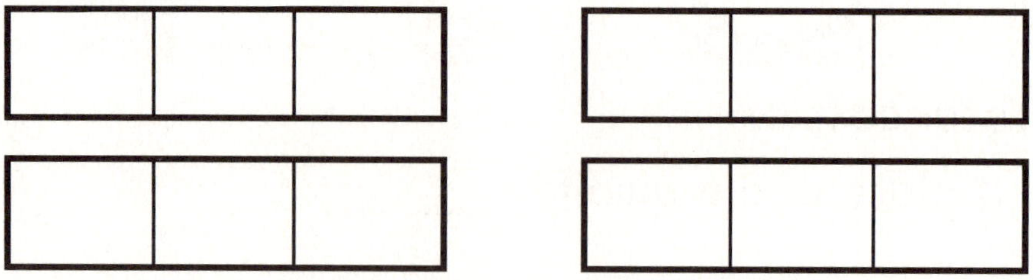

$3\frac{7}{10}$

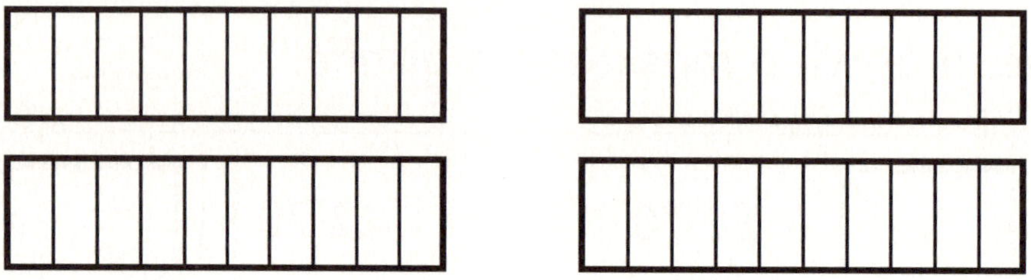

How many shapes in each set are coloured?

____

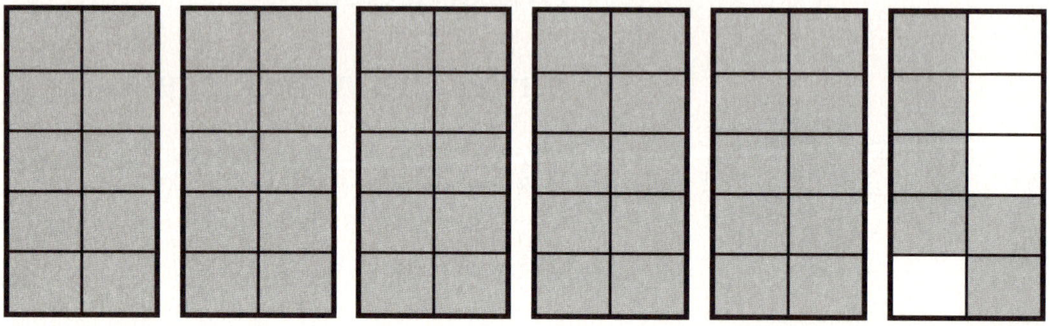

____

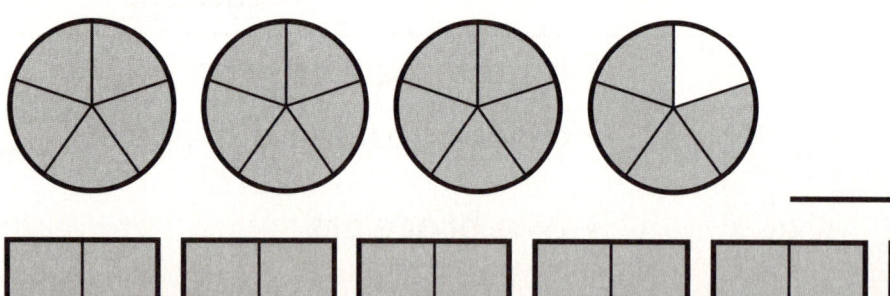

one half of 100 = ☐   one fifth of 35 = ☐

$\frac{1}{10}$ of 80 = ☐ $\frac{1}{4}$ of 36 = ☐

one third of 12 = ☐   one tenth of 10 = ☐

$\frac{1}{5}$ of 15 = ☐ $\frac{1}{3}$ of 27 = ☐

Fractions: Textbook pages 67–68

Check-up 22

Colour

one sixth 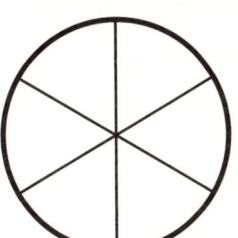 three eights 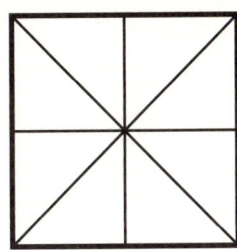 $\frac{3}{6}$ 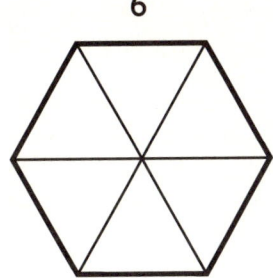 $\frac{4}{8}$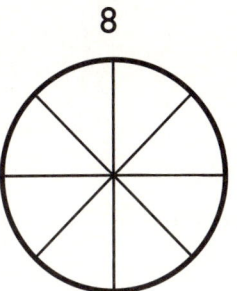

one and four sixths   two and two eighths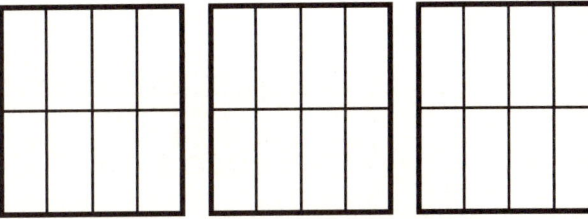

What fraction of each shape is shaded?

 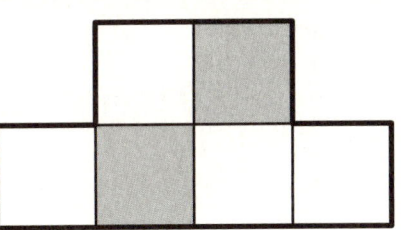

_____   _____

Colour the shapes to match each equal fractions story.

 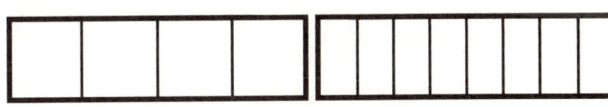

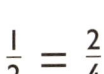 $\frac{3}{4} = \frac{6}{8}$

Complete each equal fractions story.

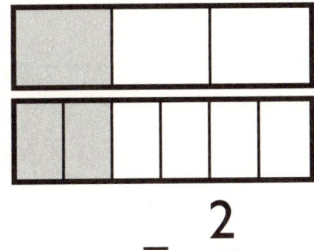 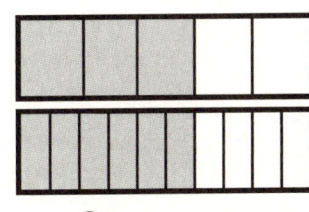

$\frac{\ }{3} = \frac{2}{\ }$ $\frac{3}{\ } = \frac{\ }{10}$

Fractions: Textbook page 69

Check-up 23

Write each time.

_____   _____   _____

_____   _____   _____

Write each time. Use am or pm.

- 10 minutes past 11 in the morning   _____

- 20 minutes to 1 in the afternoon   _____

- 7 minutes to 7 in the evening   _____

Write these times in order.
   Start with the earliest morning time.

_____ _____ _____ _____

Start with the latest evening time.

_____ _____ _____ _____

Start with the earliest time.

| 5.13pm | 9.46am | 4.27pm | 7.21am |

_____ _____ _____ _____

Time: Textbook pages 85–86

Write the time

75 minutes after

____

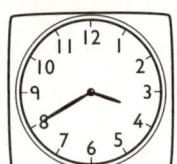

1 hour and 50 minutes after

____

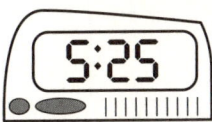

80 minutes before

____

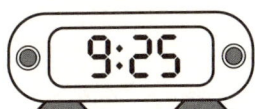

1 hour and 45 minutes before.

____

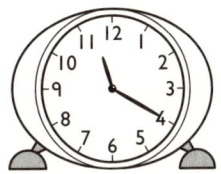

How many minutes are there between each Start time and Finish time?

Start

Finish

____

Start

Finish

____

Start

Finish

____

Start

Finish

____

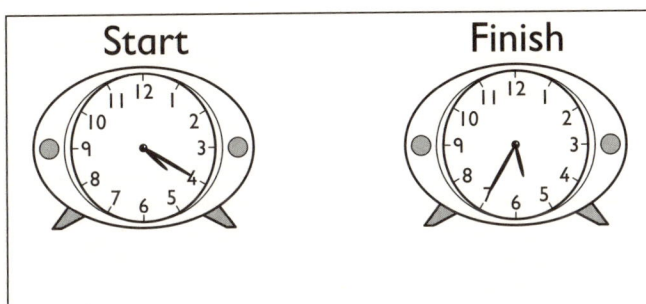

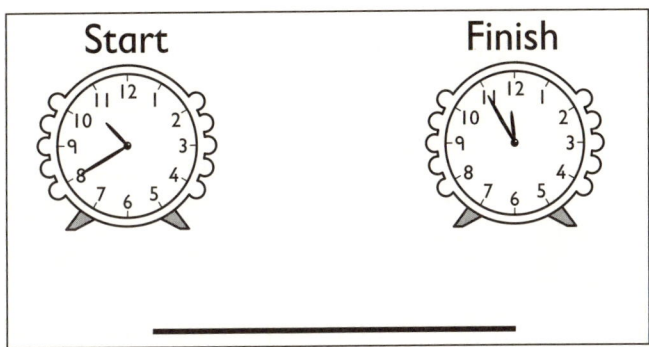

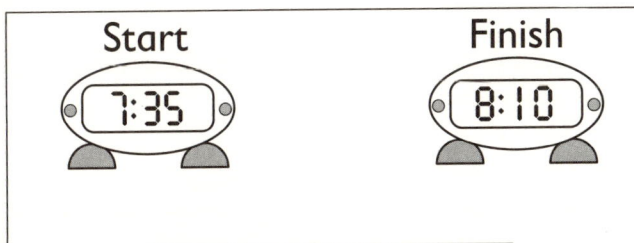

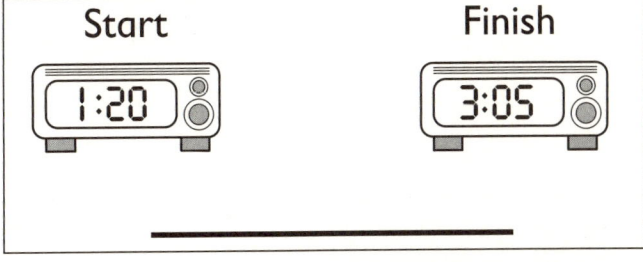

Jan left home at 9.20 am.
She jogged for 85 minutes.
When did she return home? ________

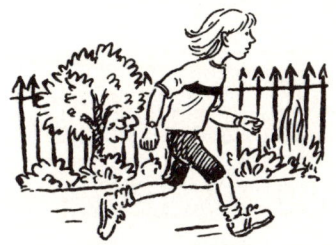

Topic Assessment
Numbers to 10 000 — 1a

1 Complete.

3960	3970	3980				
				3356	3456	3556
	1482	1481				1477
		2006	3006	4006		

2 Write the number

100 more than 6752 _____   100 less than 2764 _____

500 more than 3700 _____   1000 less than 8001. _____

3 Write a multiple of 100 between

8100 and 8500 _____   6900 and 6600. _____

Write a multiple of 1000 between

6000 and 9000 _____   10 000 and 8000. _____

4 {4758} {7548} {8475} {8547} {7584} {5847}

Write the number which has

7 tens _____   4 thousands _____   4 units _____

a hundreds digit which is double the tens digit. _____

5 Complete.

1005	Subtract 10		5007	Add 100	
4050	Subtract 100		8076	Add 1000	

Topic Assessment 1b — Numbers to 10 000

1 Write True (T) or False (F) for each example.

5987 < 6054 ____   3010 > 3001 ____   6854 < 6584 ____

2 Write in order. Start with the **smallest** amount.

£7648   £4768   £4786   £7846   £4867

____   ____   ____   ____   ____

3 Write using numerals.

Nine thousand _____   Two thousand and ten _____

Eight thousand eight hundred and two _____

Six thousand seven hundred and seventy-one _____

4 Match.

30th   50th   80th   60th

| thirtieth | sixtieth | fiftieth | eightieth |

5 Estimate about how many metres each 🐞 has crawled.

0 m ___ m   ___ m   ___ m   100 m

6 Write to the **nearest 100**.

683 ___   444 ___   962 ___

Write to the **nearest 10**.

752 ___   286 ___   995 ___

Topic Assessment
Addition to 1000

1

Double 27 = ☐   Double 46 = ☐   Double 38 = ☐

33 + 34 = ☐   29 + 28 = ☐   41 + 43 = ☐

2 Find the total of the numbers on each flag.

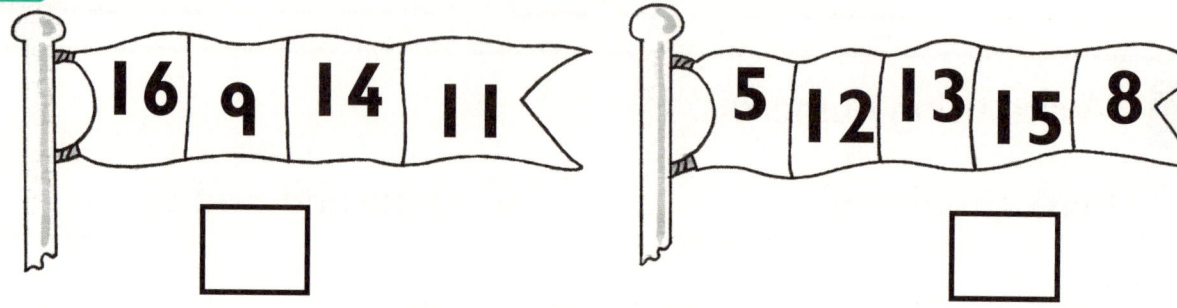

☐   ☐

3

78 + 60 = ☐   80 + 27 = ☐   90 + 63 = ☐

58 + ☐ = 108   ☐ + 70 = 145

84 + 31 = ☐   65 + 49 = ☐   71 + 68 = ☐

4

54p   35p   86p   77p   28p   65p

Find the total cost of

 and

  and

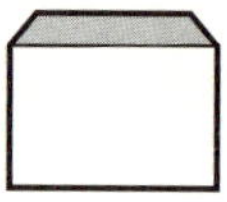

 and

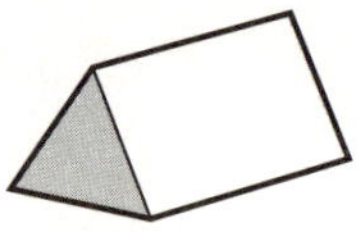

67 + ☐ = 93   ☐ + 44 = 122

Topic Assessment
Addition to 1000   2b

1

220 + 60 = ☐   420 + 70 = ☐   180 + 50 = ☐

434 + 30 = ☐   80 + 187 = ☐   676 + 40 = ☐

226 + 51 = ☐   106 + 69 = ☐   354 + 42 = ☐

2

554 + 300 = ☐   200 + 467 = ☐   509 + 400 = ☐

3 Double each number.

320 → ____   240 → ____   430 → ____

220 + 230 = ☐   170 + 160 = ☐   410 + 430 = ☐

4 How many more are needed to fill each box?

5

| Add 678 to 215. | 462 plus 375 | 458 + 467 |

Topic Assessment — Subtraction to 1000 — 3a

1

77 − 41 = ☐   86 − 22 = ☐   95 − 39 = ☐

53 − 19 = ☐   64 − 33 = ☐   48 − 29 = ☐

2

73 take away 6 ☐   65 subtract 8 ☐

5 fewer than 92 ☐   Subtract 7 from 54. ☐

Take 3 from 41. ☐   82 minus 4 ☐

3 Find the difference in price between these pots.

 and  ☐

 and  ☐

 and  ☐

The  is reduced by £14.
How much does the pot now cost? ☐

4   105 − 7 = ☐   103 − 9 = ☐   206 − 8 = ☐

362 − 5 = ☐   144 − 6 = ☐   585 − 9 = ☐

402 − ☐ = 395   ☐ − 8 = 299

Topic Assessment
Subtraction to 1000 3b

1 110 – 60 = ____   150 – 70 = ____   140 – 80 = ____

107 take away 12 ____   114 subtract 18 ____

27 fewer than 115 ____   Subtract 21 from 112. ____

Take 33 from 121. ____   126 minus 39 ____

2

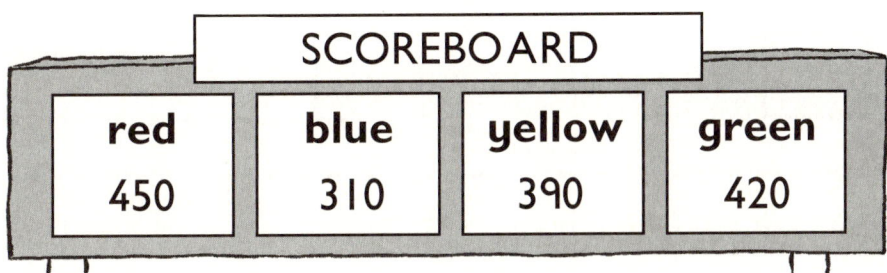

SCOREBOARD

red	blue	yellow	green
450	310	390	420

Find the difference between the scores of the

reds and yellows ____   blues and greens. ____

3 Find the difference between

96 and 103 ____   207 and 198 ____   93 and 109 ____

405 and 391 ____   488 and 505 ____   613 and 594 ____

4

683 minus 58	Subtract 327 from 386.	724 subtract 58

Topic Assessment — Multiplication 4a

1

3 × 3 = ☐   4 × 6 = ☐   8 × 2 = ☐

10 × 4 = ☐   5 × 5 = ☐   7 × 3 = ☐

5 × 8 = ☐   3 × 9 = ☐   6 × 4 = ☐

☐ × 4 = 32   ☐ × 10 = 60   ☐ × 5 = 30

5 × ☐ = 45   3 × ☐ = 12   4 × ☐ = 0

2

How many coins are in

14 packs _____   235 packs? _____

How many stamps are in

18 packs _____   72 packs? _____

10 × ☐ = 370   100 × ☐ = 2800

3

8 × 7 = ☐   3 × 6 = ☐   5 × 8 = ☐

6 × 9 = ☐   8 × 0 = ☐   6 × 6 = ☐

8 × ☐ = 32   ☐ × 6 = 6   ☐ × 8 = 48

☐   ☐   ☐

Topic Assessment — Multiplication 4b

1

9 × 2 = ☐   4 × 7 = ☐   6 × 9 = ☐

5 × 7 = ☐   9 × 9 = ☐   7 × 0 = ☐

7 × ☐ = 63   ☐ × 9 = 27   ☐ × 7 = 56

☐ × 7 = 49   9 × ☐ = 81   9 × ☐ = 36

2

4 × 17 = ☐   4 × 45 = ☐   5 × 19 = ☐

5 × 13 = ☐   20 × 40 = ☐   20 × 21 = ☐

3

4 × 80 = ☐   3 × 70 = ☐   5 × 90 = ☐

3 × ☐ = 180   4 × ☐ = 160

4 Find the cost of

3 lamps _____  £78

4 radios _____  £96

Topic Assessment — **Division** — 5a

1. Tickets for the Log Ride cost 8p each.

How many tickets can you buy for

40p ☐   72p ☐   24p ☐   56p ☐

32p ☐   80p ☐   64p ☐   48p ?☐

2.

Share 48 equally among 6. ☐   Divide 24 by 6. ☐

Group 60 in sixes. ☐   Zero divided by 6 ☐

Divide 36 equally among 6. ☐   Divide 54 by 6. ☐

3. Share equally among 9 players.

36 dominoes ☐   54 cards ☐

63 counters ☐   90 cubes ☐

☐ ÷ 9 = 5   ☐ ÷ 9 = 1

4.

14 ÷ 7 = ☐   56 ÷ 7 = ☐   35 ÷ 7 = ☐

☐ ÷ 7 = 9   ☐ ÷ 7 = 7   ☐ ÷ 7 = 0

Topic Assessment
Division 5b

1 Half of 70 _____   Divide 52 by 2. _____   Double 47 _____

Divide 120 by 2. _____ $\frac{1}{2}$ of 170 _____

Half of 960 _____ $\frac{1}{2}$ of 6000 _____

$\frac{1}{2}$ of 3800 _____   Divide 8400 by 2. _____

2  Write two division stories.

☐ ÷ ☐ = ☐   ☐ ÷ ☐ = ☐

3 7000 ÷ 10 = ☐   ☐ ÷ 10 = 900

8000 ÷ 100 = ☐   ☐ ÷ 100 = 60

4

How many cards can you buy for 96p?

_____

5

How many cards can you buy for 89p? _____

How much money do you have left? _____

6 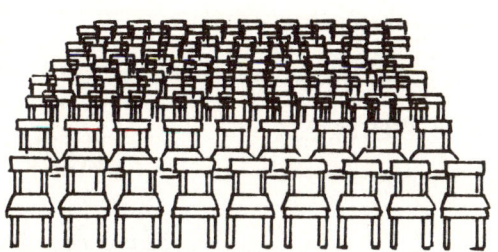 Each row has 9 seats. How many rows are needed for 59 children? _____

Topic Assessment — Money 6

1 How much?

List notes and coins to make £31·82. Use as few as possible.

☐ ☐ ◯ ◯ ◯ ◯ ◯

2 Write 5030p in pounds and pence. _____

Write £47·06 in pence. _____

3 Find the total cost of

3 masks _____

a stool and a bowl _____

2 masks and a stool _____

a lion and the beads. _____

£2·60 £2·32 £3·45 £1·58 £1·75

4 Toni and Glen each used a £20 note to buy a game. Toni's game cost £14·52. List her change.

◯ ◯ ◯ ◯ ◯ ☐

Here is Glen's change. How much did he **spend**? _____

Round these games prices to the nearest pound to **estimate** their total cost.

£7·54   £8·77   £4·23

_____

Topic Assessment — Fractions — 7

1 Colour the circles to show $2\frac{3}{5}$.

2 one fifth of 35 ☐   one quarter of 24 ☐

one third of 21 ☐   one tenth of 70 ☐

3 Colour. $\frac{5}{8}$ one and five sixths

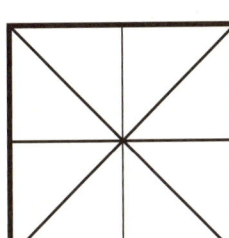 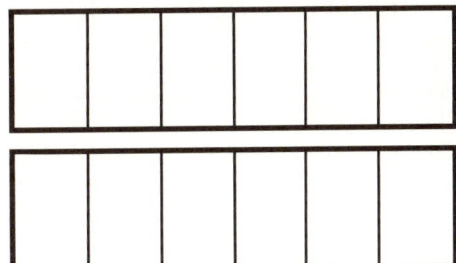

4 What fraction of this shape is shaded? ____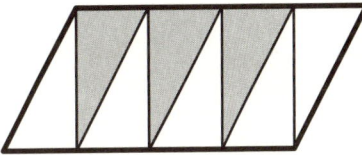

5 Colour the circles to match the equal fractions story.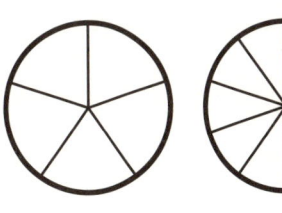

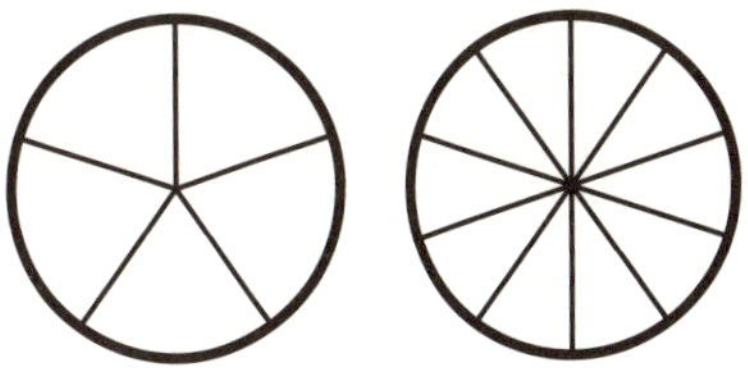

$\frac{4}{5} = \frac{8}{10}$

6 Complete the equal fractions story.

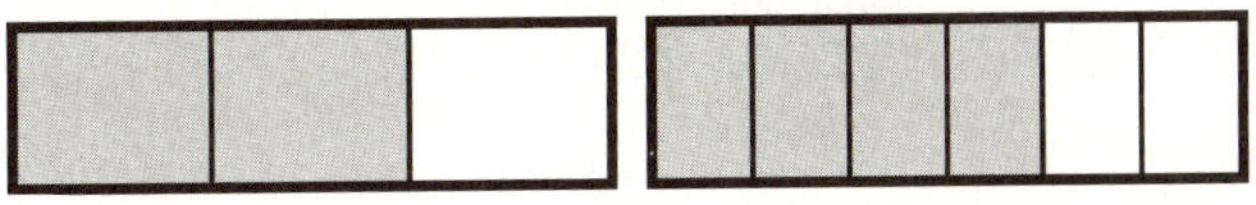

$\frac{2}{\_\_} = \frac{\_\_}{6}$

Topic Assessment — **Decimals** 8

1 Write as a decimal the fraction of the shape which is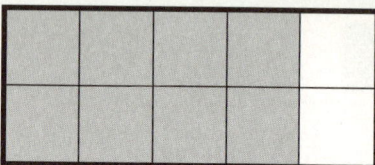

shaded _____   not shaded. _____

2 Colour the shapes to show **2·3**.

3 Write in decimal form the position shown by each arrow.

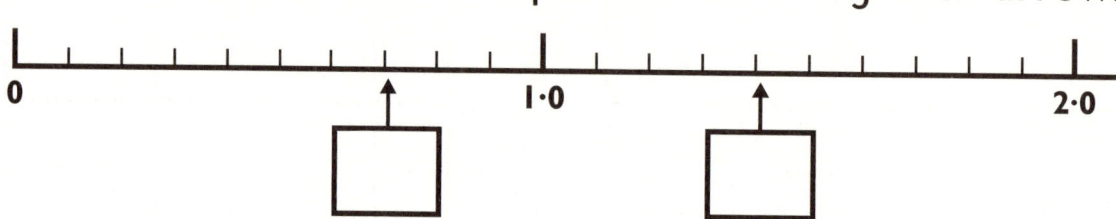

4 Write in decimal form.

$\frac{9}{10}$ _____   five tenths _____

$4\frac{1}{10}$ _____   three and six tenths _____

5 Write in order, starting with the **smallest** number.

5·0   4·8   4·0
4·5   5·4   _____ , _____ , _____ , _____ , _____

6 Roy jumped 1·7 metres.
Kim jumped 0·6 metres further than Roy.

How far did Kim jump? _____

Topic Assessment
Addition and Subtraction to 10 000 9a

1 How many points altogether have

Name	Points
Megan	900
Peter	2400
Jody	700

Megan and Jody → ____
Peter and Megan → ____
Jody and Peter → ____

800 + 500 + 300 = ☐   600 + ☐ = 1500

3600 + 700 + 200 = ☐   ☐ + 6800 = 7300

2 Double

2300 → ☐   3500 → ☐   4700 → ☐

☐ → 8000   ☐ → 4800   ☐ → 8200

3

9300 + ☐ = 10 000   ☐ + 400 = 10 000

☐ + 7500 = 8000   ☐ + 300 = 5000

4

 What is the total of 80 and 6519?
 Add 800 to 7135.

☐   ☐

Topic Assessment 9b
Addition and Subtraction to 10 000

1 1600 − 700 = ☐   2400 − 600 = ☐

6300 − 800 = ☐   1200 − 400 = ☐

2

1300 take away 9 ☐   2603 subtract 8 ☐

7 fewer than 1232 ☐   Subtract 6 from 3001. ☐

Take 4 from 3681. ☐   3724 minus 9 ☐

2375 − ☐ = 2368   ☐ − 5 = 1827

3 Find the difference between the number of boxes.

 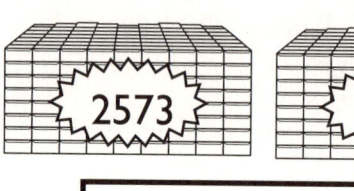

☐   ☐

Find the difference between

3004 and 2996 ☐   1998 and 2005 ☐

2658 and 2672 ☐   5003 and 4987 ☐

3006 and 2988 ☐   2011 and 1995 ☐

5603 − ☐ = 5586   ☐ − 18 = 2995

Round-up 1

1 Write the number

1 more than 8999 _____   2 less than 6010 _____

10 more than 5789 _____   100 less than 9034 _____

1000 more than 2504 _____   500 less than 5000 _____

2 Write True (T) or False (F) for each example.

6306 > 7350 ___   2975 < 2795 ___

8136 < 8163 ___   5453 > 5456 ___

3 14 + 8 + 6 + 7 = ☐   5 + 9 + 15 + 8 = ☐

4 68 + 57 = ☐   84 + 77 = ☐

36 + ☐ = 104   65 + ☐ = 121

5 Double

130 → ☐   280 → ☐   370 → ☐

6

252 + 384

178 + 243

Round-up 1

7  Sell 50. How many are left? _____

 Sell 62. How many are left? _____

8

6 × 4 = ☐   7 × 8 = ☐   9 × 6 = ☐

8 × ☐ = 48   ☐ × 6 = 36   ☐ × 9 = 72

9

4 × 32 = ☐   5 × 46 = ☐   20 × 14 = ☐

3 × 26 = ☐   4 × 90 = ☐   5 × 60 = ☐

10

Share 42 equally among 7. ☐   Divide 81 by 9. ☐

Group 45 in nines. ☐   56 divided by 7 ☐

11

6000 ÷ 10 = ☐   ☐ ÷ 10 = 300

7000 ÷ 100 = ☐   ☐ ÷ 100 = 90

Round-up 1

12  Each table can seat 6 children. How may tables are needed for 45 children? ____

13 Write
- 6045p in pounds and pence _____
- £28·60 in pence. _____

14 Alex used a £20 note to buy a book. The book cost £11·38. List his change.

○ ○ ○ ○ ○ ▭

15 $\frac{1}{4}$ of 20 = ☐   one third of 27 = ☐

$\frac{1}{10}$ of 50 = ☐   one fifth of 35 = ☐

16 Write in decimal form the position shown by each arrow.

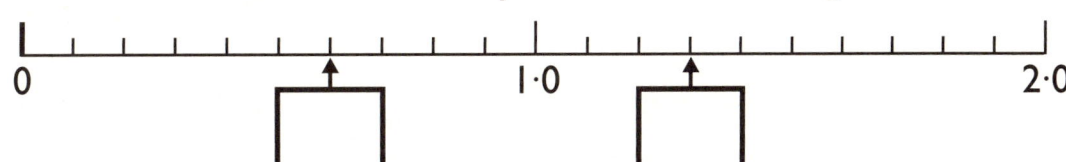

17 Write in order, starting with the smallest number.

3·4   2·3   4·3
3·3   3·2   ____ ____ ____ ____ ____

Round-up 1

18 Write each **morning** time.

_____   _____   _____

19 How many minutes are there between each Start and Finish time?

Start   Finish   Start   Finish

_____   _____

20 Write the area of this shape in square centimetres.

_____

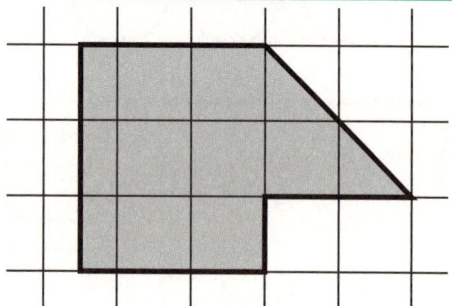

21 Tick (✓) the isosceles triangle.
Cross (✗) the equilateral triangle.

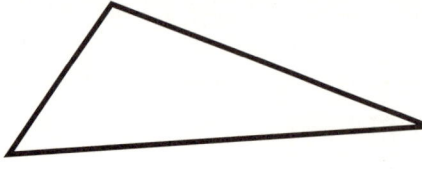 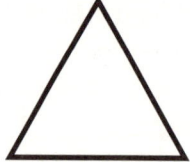 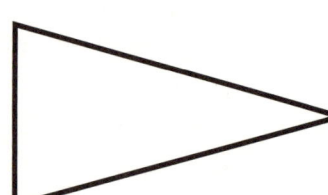

22 Write the coordinates of the

   _____

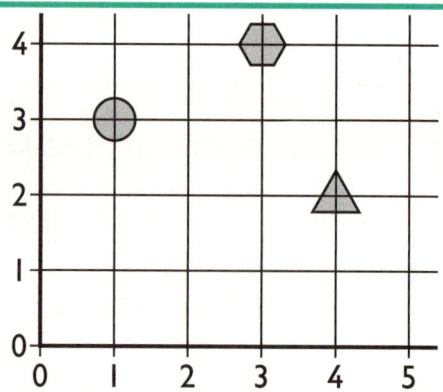

Round-up 2

1

| 8740 | 7656 | 8080 | 7564 |

Write the number which has

6 hundreds _____   8 tens _____

thousands digit 7 and units digit 4. _____

2 Write
- to the nearest 100

| 603 | | | 239 | | | 930 | |

- to the nearest 10

| 631 | | | 877 | | | 603 | |

3
76 + 60 =   90 + 27 =   82 + 50 =

34 + 81 =   56 + 69 =   65 + 72 =

4
Double 27   Double 34   Double 39   Double 46

5
 Dan £423   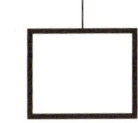 Kim £80    Li £376    Max £50

How much money altogether have

Dan and Max _____   Kim and Li? _____

Round-up 2

6 28 + ☐ = 60   37 + ☐ = 100

855 + ☐ = 900   208 + ☐ = 300

7 200 − 8 = ☐   176 − 9 = ☐   504 − 6 = ☐

865 − ☐ = 859   703 − ☐ = 695

8 150 − 70 = ☐   220 − 90 = ☐

370 − 250 = ☐   430 − 380 = ☐

9 Find the difference between

96 and 103 ☐   605 and 590 ☐

10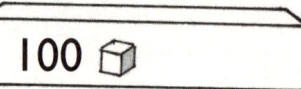

How many

◯ in 46 bags ☐   ▭ in 53 boxes? ☐

11 Find the cost of

£47   £63

4 CD players   3 pairs of trainers.

_____   _____